Old PORTPATRICK

by

J.D. Mackenzie and R.R. Cunningh...

From Schoolhouse Hill Portpatrick

Portpatrick from School House Brae, showing the old military road dropping steeply down into the village. In earlier times travellers arriving on horseback would, as they came over the brow of the hill, see the roofs of the houses so far down below them that they would appear to be below the horse's hooves. The road leading to Portpatrick in the eighteenth century was military built (the only one outwith the Highlands) and these tended to utilize early tracks which followed the high ground and avoided the woods and marshes in the valleys below. By 1774 the route from Portpatrick to Dumfries was completed and this road, with stone surfaces, side drains and culverts, was instrumental in opening up a remote and wild region.

© 1997 J.D. Mackenzie and R.R. Cunningham
First Published in the United Kingdom, 1997
Stenlake Publishing Limited, 54-58 Mill Square,
Catrine, Ayrshire KA5 6RD
www.stenlake.co.uk

ISBN 9781872074757

The Promenade, Portpatrick

Introduction

Portpatrick is a small village, but with a long history. A Stone Age ring factory was discovered on the site of new houses in Hill Street in 1901 and polished Stone Age jet rings have been found in the village.

In the earliest days, the sea was the principal support of the local economy but the combination of a relatively accessible and reliable route inland to Galloway, Scotland and England with one of the shortest sea crossings to Ireland led to the establishment of the ferry route to Ireland

Initially, there was no harbour; only the off-shore rocks gave shelter to vessels. However, by 1790 a pier and lighthouse, both designed by John Smeaton (who built Eddystone Lighthouse), were in use. This lighthouse was replaced about 1805, and the present one was completed in 1883. By the 1820s new roads had been built to Stranraer and Glasgow and to Dumfries and Carlisle, improving the mail coach and other services. At that time much of the old town was rebuilt. Construction of a new harbour was started in 1821. For this purpose a quarry, now known as Dasher's Den, was opened with a waggonway linking all the works and an Admiralty works yard, where the putting green and Welsh Place are today, was also laid out. By 1836 a new south pier, an extension of the earlier pier, with a lighthouse at the seaward end was completed; however, work on the north pier remained unfinished and stopped about 1840. These works helped to establish a regular mail and passenger service to Ireland (both of which had existed irregularly since, respectively, the sixteenth and seventeenth centuries).

Meanwhile, the reliability of the ferry service was improved by the transfer of the paddle steamers *Arrow* and *Dasher* from Dover, although the *Dasher* was wrecked in 1830. The paddle steamers *Spitfire* and *Fury* (later renamed *Asp* and *Pike)* then continued the service. However, the village's mail ferry service ceased in 1849.

The railway to Portpatrick opened in 1862 and served the harbour by a branch line from the high station. This resulted in a number of attempts to re-establish the ferry service but none lasted for long and the branch line became disused. The south pier lighthouse was dismantled in 1869, later re-erected in Colombo, Sri Lanka. The Admiralty abandoned the harbour in 1873.

A lifeboat station was established in 1877, the first lifeboat being *Civil Service No. 3*. In 1922 Portpatrick's first motor lifeboat, the *Maria*, was put into service. Lifeboats have carried out many rescues, one of the most memorable being in 1953 when the *Jeanie Speirs* went to the aid of the *Princess Victoria*. The present lifeboat is the *Mary Irene Miller*, named in 1989 by Princess Alexandra.

Since the end of the nineteenth century Portpatrick has developed as a holiday resort. Electricity came to the village in 1905 and that year the Portpatrick Hotel also opened. Around this time there was a second period of significant building and rebuilding and despite setbacks such as the closure of the railway in 1950, the expansion of the village and its amenities has continued to this day.

Portpatrick Harbour in 1815, showing the sands of the North Gullet which dried out at low tide, linking McCook Craig, on the right, to the shore. In the foreground are some of the local fishing boats and within the harbour are packet boats which sailed to and from Donaghadee since 1662.

Entering the harbour is a 'bullock boat' used for transporting black Irish cattle. Some of these boats were poorly maintained and the animals, disturbed during the crossing, occasionally caused great damage and danger by putting their hooves through the bottom or their horns through the side.

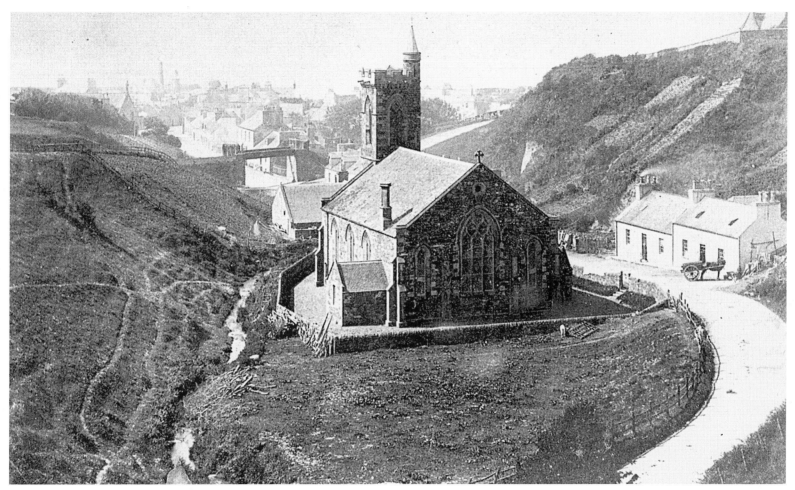

The main turnpike road from Stranraer opened in 1808 and its entry into Portpatrick was at one time known as New Street. The parish church was completed in 1842 and the open space before it was planted in 1898 to form Church Wood. On the right, the cottage with the cart outside was the Toll House. Next door was the Smithy. Further down on the right, the row of houses, Holm Street, were built in 1825. This terrace originally extended as far as Ivy Cottage, beyond the bridge, but when the harbour branch railway was built in 1862 the row was severed by the demolition of two cottages for the construction of the bridge over the road. In 1871 a third cottage was demolished for the building of Braefield Road, seen running up the hillside to the right. In 1875, the harbour branch was lifted and the openings for the bridge blocked; the bridge was removed in 1902.

A view from the North Cliff, *c.*1880, with the incomplete North Pier on the extreme right. In the foreground, on the Ward Shore, is the lifeboat house and a crane, both provided by the R.N.L.I. in 1877. At this time the lifeboat was taken out of the west gable by trolley and when launched at high tide it was pushed over a roller set in the edge of the quayside; the crane was used for retrieval of the vessel and for low tide launching. Beyond the South Pier is the quarry which supplied the whinstone for the harbour, and to the left, the houses and limekiln.

Portpatrick outer harbour, *c.*1920, showing the lighthouse of 1883. Once a thriving harbour, it is now used mainly for yachts - and during the occasional ferry strike. Such strikes have occured in 1953, 1966, 1977 and 1988. On these occasions fishing boats from Ireland came in day and night, swiftly unloading and reloading before returning to their home ports. The lorries that supplied the boats rumbled by at all hours and a few of the holiday home owners, mostly retired people who thought they had come to a quiet, peaceful village, objected to the noise and the mess left by the whole operation. They were all too thankful when the strike finally ended.

MAIN STREET, PORTPATRICK.

Main Street at the beginning of the twentieth century, looking north from Harbour Square. This street was built around 1800 and cut through much of the site of the former monastic buildings. On the right is the Downshire Arms Hotel, raised to four stories in 1893 but retaining the skews at the new roof level. Next is the Cross Keys Inn. Beside this are shops, including Miss Brown's Sweet Shop. Next to it was a bank, later the Post Office. On the left a short row mostly contained shops. Each end house was semi-circular, the nearest end here having been removed. Today, there are no shops on the right and the Cross Keys has merged with the Downshire Arms. Of the row on the left, the nearest shop was a chemist in the 1950s, and was also once a branch of the Royal Bank of Scotland.

Johnny Patterson of Low Merrick Farm ('Johnny the Merrick') delivering milk to the Commercial Inn in Main Street, early 1900s. He brought the milk round every morning on a spring cart pulled by Daisy the horse and customers provided their own jugs into which the milk was ladled. Ivy Cottage, built in 1825, is beyond the Commercial Inn. Unfortunately, it lost its distinguishing feature in the severe winter of 1963.

The Bell Tower of St Andrew's, or the Auld Kirk, possibly dates from the Celtic period when the site was known as Chapel Patrick. As the Roman Catholic religion in Scotland displaced the Celtic, so a Roman Catholic church was built on the site, and the opening of the aumbrey hole can still be seen in the wall at the east end of the church. In 1628 the Parish of Portpatrick was formed and the then ruined church was rebuilt to become the parish kirk. A new church was built in 1842 but the tower remained as the graveyard around it was still in use, although it was replaced later that century. The tower was renovated in 1984 and the old bell was placed in the parish church.

The Free Church as seen from Dinvin Street, *c.*1905. This was built in 1844 around the original of 1843. In 1887 a tower with a spire and vestry was added and in 1903 a set of melodious tuned chimes were installed in the tower. In 1929, following the Union of the Churches, services were held in both the Parish and former Free Churches, but in June 1935 services in the former Free Church ceased. After being requisitioned during the Second World War, the building became a plumbers premises and in 1952 was repurchased for use as the church hall. The vestry was used by Wigtown County Council as the branch library until superseded by the present mobile library in the 1970s. The spire and chimes were removed about 1964.

Sea Front Portpatrick.

A view of the South and North Crescents, *c.*1923. Prior to 1820, the beach sloped up to the road which was known as Shore Street. When the harbour was enlarged the present esplanade was built by the Admiralty at the approximate high tide mark to provide a level route for a waggonway to carry quarried stone to and from the various harbour works. An incidental result of the building of the esplanade was the rebuilding of some of the Shore Street houses, as they could now be moved a little closer to the sea. By the mid-nineteenth century the names South and North Crescents had come into use. On abandoning the harbour, the Admiralty refused to carry out any more maintenance on the esplanade and as a result a severe gale in 1884 breached the esplanade wall supporting South Crescent and destroyed the slipway at the end of the South Pier. Eventually the roads department had to make good the damage, but the slipway (still in use today) was not replaced until seven years later.

Portpatrick beach, 1912. Modelled on the cottage at the top left, the sandcastle was made by Dr Carroll of the Royal Northern School of Music who built them every summer to collect funds for the R.N.L.I. The girl posing proudly beside it is his daughter.

Lifeboat Day, 1910, with the *Civil Service No.3* on exercise. This was the second lifeboat with that name to be stationed in the port and between 1900 and 1924 it was launched 18 times, saving 42 lives. Lifeboat Day was always an occasion of entertainment and funds were collected while the lifeboat and its crew carried out various manoeuvres to demonstrate its capabilities. In 1907 the main door of the lifeboat house was moved to the east end and a new crane was placed in front of the fish sheds. To their right is the grain store and next to it the small building, built about 1876, which housed the Rocket Apparatus. The path to Sandeel Bay zig-zags up the north cliff behind and on the clifftop is the mast of the radio station.

A rocket life saving exercise, *c.*1900. The local Coast Guard was established during the nineteenth century, taking over a cottage in Dunskey Street which backed onto the sea, thus giving them a good look-out. In 1863, Dennett's Rocket Life Saving Apparatus, later known as the 'breeches buoy', was installed at the station.

The apparatus consisted of a light line attached to a rocket which was fired over the wreck. Once attached to the stricken vessel, this line was used to pull out a heavier line, which in turn hauled out the main rope which carried the breeches buoy. The intermediate line was then used as a hauling line to shuttle the breeches buoy to and from the wreck, thus bringing all the shipwrecked persons ashore.

The equipment was at first kept near to the Coast Guard at the south end of the village, but in 1876 a specially constructed building was erected at the north end of the west side of the inner basin. Many people were rescued using this apparatus and in 1963 a centenary demonstration was held. However, in 1992, despite local opposition, all rescue equipment held by the Coast Guard at Portpatrick was removed, and a replacement unit set up at Stranraer.

Stranded Steamer "Tyrconnel," Ward Shore, Portpatrick

Winter gales in the area can be severe enough to endanger even vessels within the harbour. In December 1894 the steamer *Strathspey* grounded in fog at Saltpans Bay, about 5 miles to the north, and to help in its recovery the salvage steamer *Seamew* was dispatched to Portpatrick. Three weeks later a heavy storm caused the *Seamew* to brake free from her moorings in the harbour and the ship was driven across to the south beach at the foot of Barrack Street. Scarcely had she got stuck in the sand when it was found that another steamer was sitting on the rocks of the Ward Shore abreast of the lifeboat house. The nine-man crew of the *Tyrconnel*, as the vessel proved to be, were speedily brought ashore by the rocket brigade. The ship is seen here well and truly stranded. To free her the boulders below the vessel were blown apart to allow launching tracks to be laid. Four months later she was successfully refloated but the *Seamew* and *Strathspey* did not fare as well. Both were totally wrecked.

A view from the west, 1903, showing the terrace of houses in Blair Street under construction. The tennis courts and bowling green occupied part of the site of the former Harbour Station, which was at the foot of the cliffs close to the inner basin. Initially, land for the tennis court, which opened in 1890, was rented from the railway company as was land for a bowling green which opened three years later. This photograph was taken from the North Cliff footpath which continues about one mile along the coast to Sandeel Bay, which is very popular for bathing. This now forms part of the route of the Southern Upland Way which was established in 1984 and runs from Portpatrick on the Irish Sea, to Cockburnspath on the North Sea.

The club house of the golf course was built on the original road between the village and Dunskey House. Officially opened in June 1903, the course was built upon the grounds known as Kennel Park and also much of the Mill Field, combining to create an area in excess of 100 acres. In 1904 a ladies club house was added. The course was rearranged in 1914 to take in part of Cove Hill and other ground along the cliff top, and some golfers have found it necessary to drive out to sea during windy days in the hope that the ball will land somewhere further up the fairway!

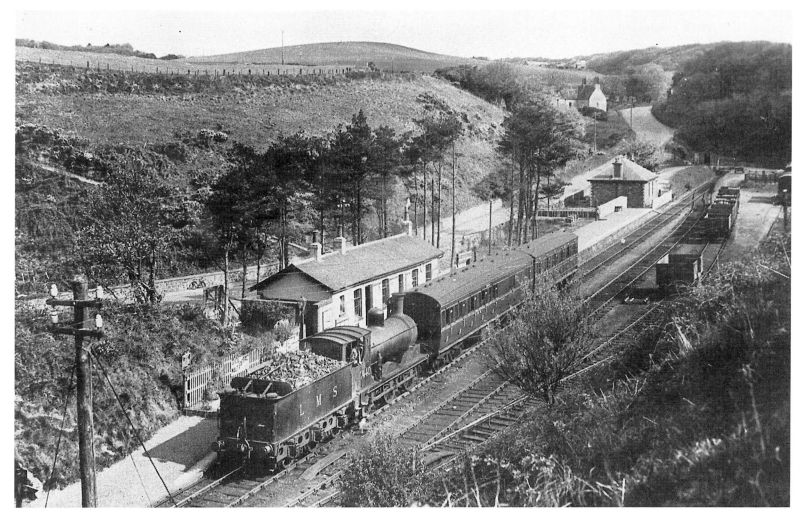

The railway station, 1930s. The railway to Portpatrick was opened in August 1862 by the Portpatrick Railway Company which was only independent for a further two years until the Caledonian Railway took over the line. In 1885 the Portpatrick railway was vested jointly between the London & North Western, Midland, Caledonian and Glasgow & South Western Railways; the branch became part of the Portpatrick & Wigtownshire Joint Railway. Shown is an ex-C.R. goods locomotive, one of a type generally known as 'Jumbo's'.

The railway followed a coastal route, before turning east and inland to the station. The loco shed, bottom left, seems to have been little used as most trains worked to and from Stranraer throughout the period of the line's use. After the line was closed in 1950, the station became a caravan site and the old buildings were retained as the ablutions block. In 1992 the area was completely cleared for housing development.

Landing cod in the inner basin, *c*.1905. At this time, fishing was done in both rowing and sailing boats and these were usually manned by a crew of three. The cod were caught by the long-line method during a season lasting from November to April when they headed southwards. The bait was the shell-fish *Buccunum Undatum*, or 'Buckie', and this was used with lines up to 6000ft long, with hooks every 6ft and held on the sea bed by large stones. The ends were marked by buoys on the surface. The fishermen were selective, the smallest fish not being taken as the largest fish could weigh around 40lbs. The introduction of trawlers in the late 1920s, locally called the 'vacuum cleaners of the seas', led to the elimination of this method of fishing.

Sorting cod in front of the lifeboat house, before the alterations were made to it in 1907. Portpatrick was once one of the biggest exporters of cod to London and after the fish were sorted, they were boxed and taken by cart to the railway station. On one occasion a fisherman accompanying the catch to Stranraer, having had an early celebration of his catch at the pub, asked the train crew not to shunt at Colfin as he would be having a nap. He promised a tip of £2 - "Oh, Aye," the engine driver replied doubtfully. The fisherman fell fast asleep and the train duly got to Colfin, shunting as usual. Upon arriving at Stranraer Town station, the fisherman roused himself, went to the train crew and expressing his pleasure at such a smooth journey gave them the £2.

Steamships have been calling at Portpatrick ever since their introduction and by the 1820s there was a thrice weekly service of steamers between Liverpool and Greenock, calling at the Isle of Man and Portpatrick *en route*. Apart from the packet boats to Ireland, the steamships tended to be excursion vessels such as the one pictured, *c*.1890. However, as vessels got bigger, they became too large for the inner basin of the harbour and most services stopped.

A late-nineteenth century view of the steam yacht *Queen Margaret*, her funnel capped and lifeboats removed for the winter. The boat was owned by E.H. Gaskell of London, who employed villagers as her crew. These included the captain, Samuel Vint, who looked after the vessel in the winter and commanded it during summer cruises with Mr Gaskell and his family and friends. Perched on top of a rock overlooking the harbour on the left is the Knowe Cottage, built in the mid-1890s by the Vints who were all deep-sea sailors. Following the death of Mr Gaskell, the *Queen Margaret* was sold in February 1899 and taken out of Portpatrick for the last time. Subsequently Vint and his crew were in charge of the yacht *Dandelion* and then crewed the racing yachts owned by Dr Inglis of Pointhouse, enjoying many successful seasons on and around the Clyde Coast.

Dunskey Castle is about a half mile to the south and reached by the cliff top path which goes on to Morroch Bay. Although its origins are unknown, it was from here that the local estate was administered prior to the building of Dunskey House and it was once in the possession of the Adair family who still own lands in Northern Ireland. Often described as a sixteenth century L plan tower house, the tower is actually built into a much older courtyard castle, complete with sea gate and vallum (or dry ditch) and, on the landward side, a moat which still holds water. In 1648 The Rev. James Blair purchased the estate, then known as Portree, and renamed it Dunskey Estate. It is said that his wife did not like living quite so close to the sea and so the decision was taken to build a new house to the north of Portpatrick, the present Dunskey House. The castle was abandoned and stripped of all cut stone, timber and other valuable material, so that by 1684 it was a ruin.

The first mention of a Dunskey House was in the late seventeenth century and it is said to have been partly constructed from materials from a priest's house wrecked during the Reformation. These included a beam which is supposed to have carried a curse that no Laird of Dunskey would pass from father to son. For a time it seemed to have had an effect, although now the curse appears to have lost its potency.

The structure of the house was altered over the years but today's imposing structure, completed in 1903, was the result of improvements in the Baronial style which meant the virtual demolition of the former house. In this last rebuilding the cursed beam was removed and left in the Old Kirk Yard, where it gradually disappeared as the villagers chopped it up for firewood.

* Dunskey House and grounds are privately owned and not open to the public.

The Heather House in Dunskey Glen, which extends from Laird's Bay (Port Kale on the map) almost to Dunskey House. One of the most picturesque glens in Galloway, it is distinguished by a footpath that allows glimpses of the valley and the sea, and passes a waterfall crossed by a rustic bridge. The Heather House provided a welcome place to stop and admire the view and although it is long gone, the walk remains.

At Laird's Bay the double-hexagonal cable house of 1854 can still be seen although the undersea cable was removed in 1983, replaced by one running through the adjacent Sandeel Bay. In 1995 Major Orr-Ewing, the Laird of Dunskey, converted the old cable house into a Coastal Interpretation Centre, with displays of shells, rock formations and wildlife.

Mrs Galloway and Mr Smith of Morroch Bay. This is about one and a half miles to the south and was a popular destination for day trips in the late Victorian and Edwardian periods. These trips were often made by boat as the land route was along dangerous cliff tops. The bay itself is sandwiched between cliffs and the sea, and contains a smallholding, the path down to which is extremely steep and narrow. In the 1870s this smallholding was a 'black house', so called as it had few windows and no chimney. The smoke from the fire escaped through a hole in the roof.

Morroch Bay has seen its share of shipwrecks such as the SS *Lurcher* in 1920, which ran aground in fog, miraculously missing the surrounding rocks. The passengers were taken to Portpatrick and many locals turned out to help rescue the cargo of 150 cattle and horses. Later, the ship was successfully refloated.

The extension of the Heugh Road towards the sea commenced in 1903, allowing a number of new villas to be built on the north side of the village. Most of these were completed by 1907, including the Factor's house, shown here around the 1920s. Subsequently, it became a private house and after World War Two a hotel known as 'Rickwood' which is still in business today.

The old Portpatrick school was built in 1862 as the parish church school and became the parish school in 1873 when school boards were established. The building was very close to the railway and after this closed in 1950, the cutting behind the school was filled in for construction of the playing field. In 1977 this field provided the site for the new school. Here the old and new (which won an architectural award) are viewed together from Braefield Road; the old school was demolished in 1979.

In 1913, the steamship *Dunira* broke down near the Isle of Man and was being towed from Ramsey to Greenock for repairs when disaster struck. As they approached Portpatrick the tow rope parted and distress flares were set off. The lifeboat was launched, and the Rocket Apparatus set up along the cliff top. Battling through heavy seas the lifeboat approached the *Dunira* and after the steamer dropped anchor the ships engineer and mate jumped to safety in the worsening weather. However, the anchor cable broke and the ship drifted rapidly shorewards with the lifeboat following. Despite being dashed against the ship twice, the skillful handling of the lifeboat by Coxswain James Smith enabled the rest of the crew to be rescued. The *Dunira* was not so lucky and was smashed upon the South Witch Rocks not far from Dunskey Castle.

Civil Service No.3 and her crew outside the lifeboat house, c.1909. This lifeboat was much larger than the first one and although alterations were made to the lifeboat house, difficulties remained and it wasn't until five years later that a cradle and rails were provided for easier movement of the boat to the crane. In 1922 the *Civil Service No.3* was replaced by the motor lifeboat *Maria*.

Portpatrick Bowling Club, Closing Day, 1915.

The bowling club on its closing day in 1915. The green was opened in 1893 and the clubhouse was completed in 1899.

A double-headed twelve coach excursion train climbs out of the village, *c.*1924. Trains of this length were not easy to handle in Portpatrick station as the platform could only hold six coaches. However, the village was always a favourite destination for excursions trains; indeed the first of these services were run within a few days of the line being opened and they continued until 1949.

In the foreground is the lifeboat *Maria* which was in service for 7 years. It was launched 10 times, saving 6 lives, and was the boat that started the tradition of taking visitors for a short sail on Lifeboat Day.

The platform, late 1920s. The station was initially very basic, but improvements were made over the years such as the construction of a footpath to the village in 1905. Today, nothing remains of the station in Portpatrick itself but the signal box is still in use; when the signals were removed in 1934 it was stored and recommissioned at Barrhill a year later.

In December 1929 the lifeboat *Maria* was replaced by the *J&W*. The naming ceremony, pictured here, took place in 1931 and the Duke of Montrose presented certificates to two retired coxswains of the lifeboat; James Smith, who had been a member of the crew for 44 years and cox for 17 until his retirement in 1930, and James Hunter, who had served for 23 years, and was cox for 6.

The *J&W* at her moorings in the inner basin during her stay from 1929 to 1937. The motor lifeboats were kept permanently afloat at moorings in the inner basin and the crew used a dinghy for boarding. The *J&W* was launched 14 times and saved 27 lives.

Holm St Portpatrick.

The village, looking south, *c.*1925, and showing Holm Street, Main Street beyond the remains of the old bridge, and Braefield Road going up the hill to the right. On the left side of Holm Street beyond the Parish Church is the Police Station and its garden, then extending almost to the old bridge; this was the site of the old people's houses built in 1965. Holm Street contained, amongst other shops, Wallace's sweet shop at the end of the row and next to it Gibb Bros who sold ladies clothing and accessories. Both were later taken over by Nancy Paterson, who continues to sell ladies clothing and now has the only shop in Holm Street. In the foreground is the Stranraer bus, a service which began in 1924.

Harbour Square, *c.*1908. The house on the extreme left, known as Anglesea, contained the town office for the Portpatrick Hotel and at one time was a working men's club. To its right is the prominent two storey building, Rockville, built in the 1770s as the Government House, and to the right again, in the centre, is the Downshire Arms. The small building in front of the Downshire Arms is now two cottages. In the late-nineteenth century the furthermost cottage was Alex Rankin's Ladies & Gents Outfitters where clothing was hand-made in the shop by tailors who could be seen at work through the front window. Subsequently, it became Mrs Brook's sweet shop and then Willy Stevenson's tea room. In the other cottage Mrs Leich made plum duff and sold it for 1d per slice, but by 1900 the house was the Victoria Coffee House.

MAIN STREET, PORTPATRICK.

Harbour Square in the late 1940s. On the right is Young's the Grocers which in 1985 became the Auld Acquaintance Cafe and eleven years later the Old Port Pantry. Next to it is the former Railway Inn and then Gillespie's the bakers, who came to Portpatrick in 1884.

PORTPATRICK

D 2676

A general view of the village, *c*.1955. The putting green in the foreground was the site of Wigtownshire's first shipyard, established about 1790 by Sir James Hunter-Blair. From 1821 this was the site of the Admiralty works yard for the new harbour and the flagstaff in the putting green dates from this period. Behind is Blair Terrace, numbers three and four of which were combined during the Second World War to accommodate USAF personnel billeted in the village. To the right of the putting green is Knowe Cottage, and partly hidden behind it are the buildings of the Blair Arms, Portpatrick's first inn. While touring Great Britain in 1698, Tsar Peter the Great of Russia stayed here on his way to Ireland and the room in which he slept is still known as the Emperor's Room.

Dirk Bogarde, with his six year old co-star Jon Whitely, chats with Mrs McCracken who at that time was one of the village's oldest inhabitants. Bogarde was starring in the film *Hunted*, a modern day version of *Kidnapped*, and in 1951 Portpatrick was chosen for a location as the script called for the involvement of a herring fleet. Each day filming was watched by crowds of onlookers and many of them, including most of the local children, were taken on as extras. On one occasion the extras had spent the day hanging around with very little to do and finally they were told that they would not in fact be required until the next day. Rather annoyed by this, they declined to follow this instruction and the film company had to bring in new recruits from Stranraer. They were told to act as fishermen. but not knowing exactly what to do they were soon being advised by the locals.

HARBOUR AND PORTPATRICK HOTEL.

The *Adoration*, which appeared in *Hunted*, beached for cleaning and painting in the outer harbour, *c.*1950. The sands here are often used for this and most of the local boats, including the lifeboat, are usually cleaned once a year. On occasion, the beached boats have been used by photographers as picturesque backgrounds for clothing catalogue shoots.

The lifeboat *Jeanie Speirs* being named in 1937. At Portpatrick she was launched 66 times and saved 18 lives. During the War she was often called out to search for casualties, such as in 1944 when a Dakota ambulance plane *en route* from Normandy to Prestwick flew into the cliffs at Cairngarroch Bay four miles to the south. There were no survivors and next day the lifeboat took on the grim task of recovering the bodies. In the winter of 1947, heavy snowfall blocked both road and railway to the village, and the lifeboat had to go to Stranraer for the rations.

Portpatrick

The boat entering the harbour is the *Seagull* which carried guests from the inner basin to the house, 'Knockinaam', which stood by the sea two miles to the south. The inner basin is overlooked by the Portpatrick Hotel which opened for the summer of 1905. Building took two years and it had to be further extended in 1907.

The fishing fleet of the 1950s was comprised mainly of traditional fishing boats which followed the herring shoals around the Scottish coast and used Portpatrick as their base in the autumn. Herring catches could be enormous and often the whole of the inner basin was used by the fleet for unloading. There was no fishing on Sundays, and occasionally so many boats were moored in the harbour that it was possible to walk across without getting wet. This was sometimes useful, for once when a local merrymaker fell into the harbour, two local boys jumped down on to the moored fishing boats and, scrambling from boat to boat, reached the fellow struggling in the water without having to risk going into it themselves.

The centenary celebrations of Portpatrick Lifeboat were held in 1977. Many events and demonstrations took place, and here a rocket line is being fired from the lifeboat during a demonstration of different rescue methods. These celebrations set the pattern for subsequent lifeboat weeks which commenced in 1979.

In 1904 the Coast Guard station moved from the south end of the village to the site of the Volunteers Fort on the North Cliff. Portpatrick Coast Guard were responsible for all shipping movements in not only the Northern Irish Sea but also the Clyde and Western Approaches, but this responsibility was downgraded to storm watch only when the new headquarters at Ardrossan were opened. In this 1930s picture the look-out is the building on the extreme right. In 1905 additional buildings had been erected here for the installation of wireless telegraphy and with the downgrading of the Coast Guard operation, the radio station took over most of the site The look-out survived until the 1980s and the radio station now occupies all the buildings.

The *Craigantlet*, bound from Belfast to Liverpool, ran aground across the mouth of Port-a-Maggie Bay in February 1982. Because of the heavy seas, the lifeboat could not take the crew off so a Sea King helicopter was called to rescue them. Pounded by the swell, the ship broke her back a few days later and containers containing toxic waste escaped from the hold and washed ashore. It was September before the bay was cleared.

The First and Last Milestone, just outside Portpatrick on the road to Stranraer. The milestone was erected in 1808 when the turnpike (toll) road opened and an iron plate attached to it gave the distances to London, Dumfries, Stranraer and Portpatrick itself. Tolls were abolished in 1865, leaving only the milestones as a relic of this period.